How do they work?

Construction Toys

Wendy Sadler

Heinemann Library
Chicago, Illinois

Customer Service 888-454-2279
Visit our website at www.heinemannlibrary.com

Editorial: Andrew Farrow and Dan Nunn
Design: Ron Kamen and Dave Oakley/Arnos Design
Picture Research: Hannah Taylor
Production: Duncan Gilbert

Originated by Ambassador Litho Ltd
Printed and bound in China by South China Printing Company.

09 08 07 06 05
10 9 8 7 6 5 4 3 2 1

Library of Congress Cataloging-in-Publication Data
Sadler, Wendy.
  Construction toys / Wendy Sadler.
    p. cm. -- (How do they work?)
  Includes bibliographical references and index.
  ISBN 1-4034-6826-5 (library binding-hardcover) -- ISBN 1-4034-6832-X (pbk.)
  1. Building--Juvenile literature. 2. LEGO toys--Juvenile literature. I. Title. II. Series.
  TH149.S235 2005
  688.7'25--dc22

                    2004020543

Acknowledgements
The publishers would like to thank the following for permission to reproduce photographs:
Alamy Images (Pat Behnke) p. **13**; Corbis (Dave G. Houser) p. **29**; Getty Images (Robert Harding) p. **28**; Harcourt Education Ltd (Tudor Photography) pp. **4**, **6**, **7**, **8**, **9**, **10**, **11**, **12**, **14**, **15**, **16**, **17**, **18**, **19**, **20**, **21**, **22**, **23**, **24**, **25**, **26**, **27**; Rex Features (TIM) p. **5**.

Cover photograph reproduced with permission of Harcourt Education Ltd (Tudor Photography).

The paper used to print this book comes from sustainable resources.

Contents

Some words are shown in bold, **like this**. You can find out what they mean by looking in the glossary.

Construction Toys

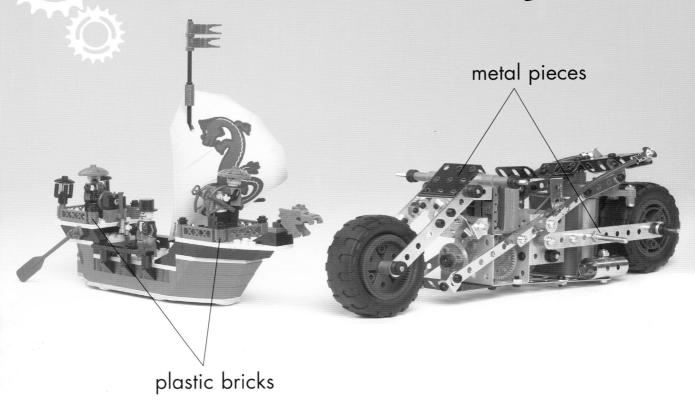

metal pieces

plastic bricks

You can make almost anything you like using **construction** toys! Some construction toys use plastic bricks. Others are made of metal and use **nuts** and **bolts** to hold them together.

Some building toys have moving parts. This giant dinosaur model was made by putting lots of smaller pieces together.

5

Building Bricks

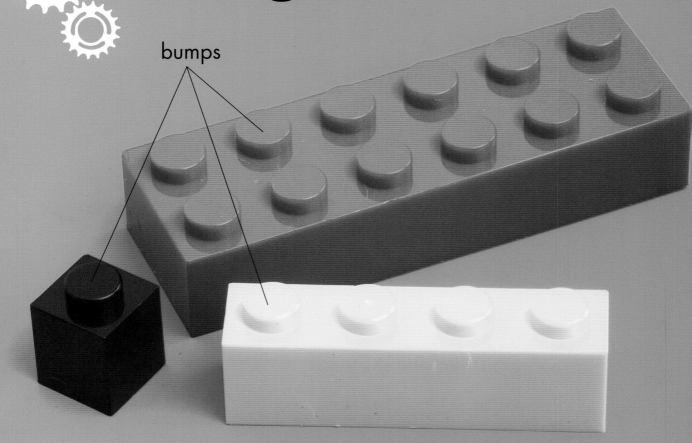

bumps

These are building bricks. They come in different shapes and sizes. All of the bricks have bumps on the top.

Bricks can be joined together to make
bigger shapes. The bumps on top of each
brick fit into the bottom of other bricks.
By putting the bricks together you can
make a strong wall or tower.

Making Shapes

Bricks can be put together to make many shapes. Square and rectangular bricks can be built into a slope or triangle shape. The rows of bricks get shorter as you build higher.

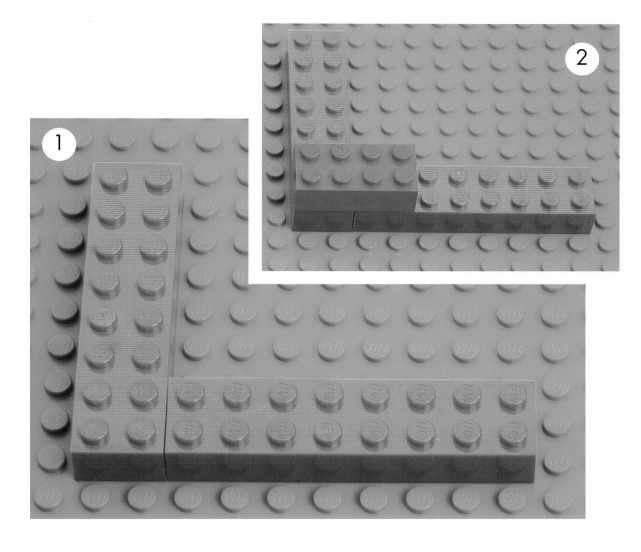

Bricks can be used to make corners.
First put two bricks together in the shape
of a letter "L." Then put another brick
over the top of them to join the two
bricks together.

9

Bricks That Do Things

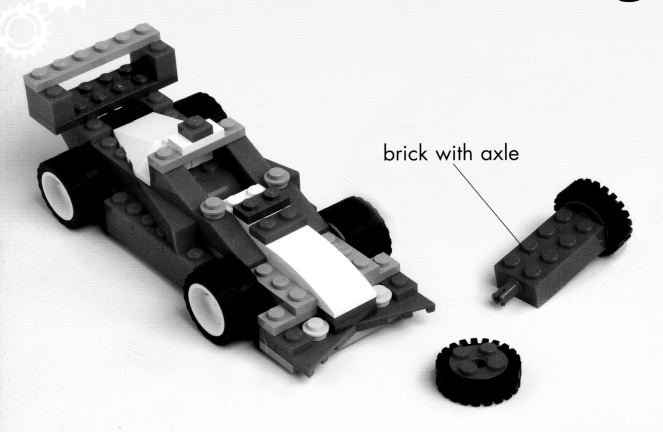

brick with axle

Some bricks have moving parts. The brick
on the right of this photo has an **axle** in
it. You can put wheels on the axle and
use the brick to make a car.

The arms move.

The eyes light up.

Some bricks use **electricity** to do different things. They can move, light up, or even make sounds! The bricks in this monkey toy get their electricity from **batteries**.

The battery inside the brick provides electricity.

Making Big Models

You can make very big models
by using lots and lots of bricks.
To make this model you need lots
of different-shaped bricks.

This model lion uses lots of big bricks. The finished model is even bigger than a child!

Rods and Connectors

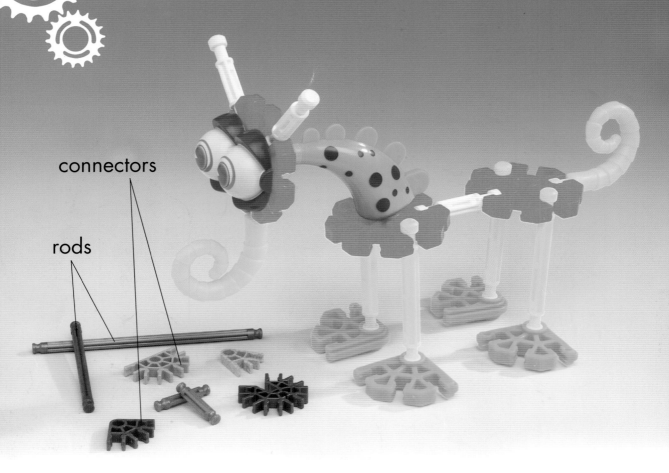

connectors

rods

This toy is made of **rods** and **connectors**. Rods are long, thin poles. Connectors join things together. There are rods of different lengths. There are also different kinds of connectors.

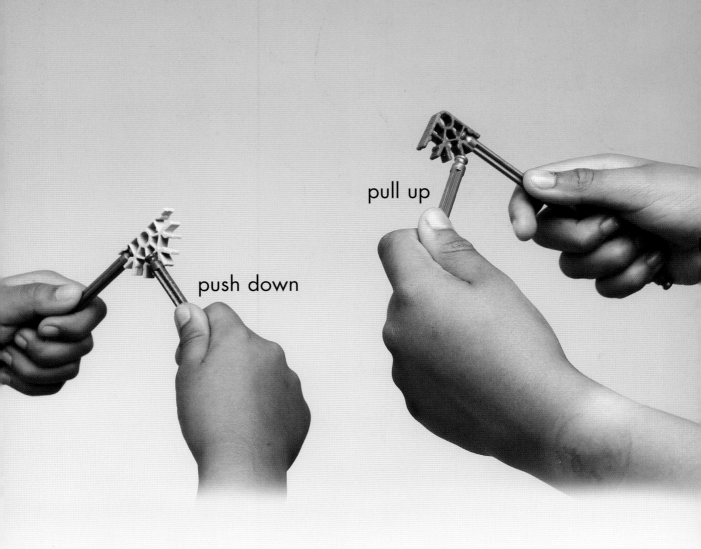

push down

pull up

You can join rods together by pushing the ends into a connector. Each rod clicks into place. You can take a rod out again by pulling it.

15

Making Shapes with Rods

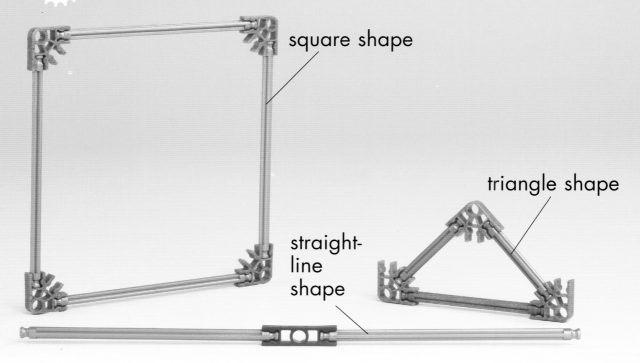

square shape

triangle shape

straight-line shape

By pushing **rods** into different parts of a **connector**, you can make different shapes. These connectors have been used to make square, triangle, and straight-line shapes.

twist

You can use lots of rods and connectors to make a really big model. Sometimes you need to turn or twist the rods to make them fit together.

Models with Wheels

An **axle** is a **rod** that holds a wheel and lets it turn around. The rods of this model can be used as axles. The wheels are pushed on to the rods and then built into the buggy.

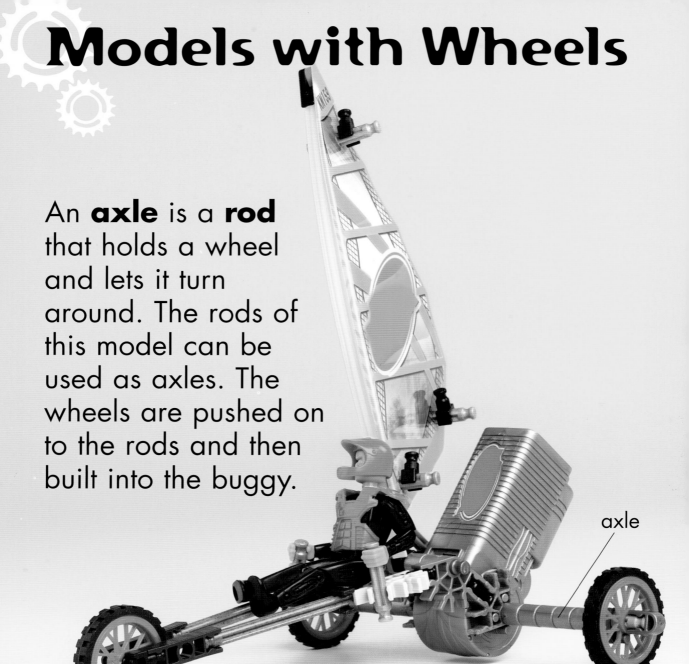

axle

wheels turn

push

When the buggy is pushed, the wheels turn. This means the buggy can move forward.

How Things Move

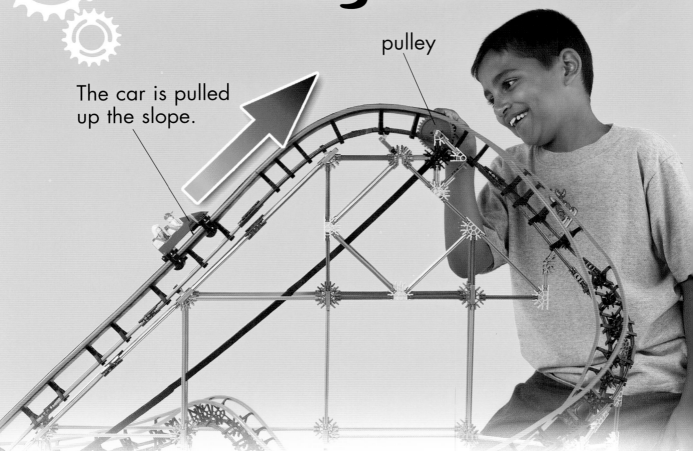

The car is pulled up the slope.

pulley

A **pulley** is a wheel with string going around it. The pulley on this model roller coaster is used to pull the car up the slope. When the wheel is turned, the string lifts the car up.

Gravity pulls the car down.

Gravity pulls everything towards the ground. Gravity is pulling this car down the slope of the roller coaster. The car is going so fast that it will not need to be pulled up the next slope.

Connecting Pieces

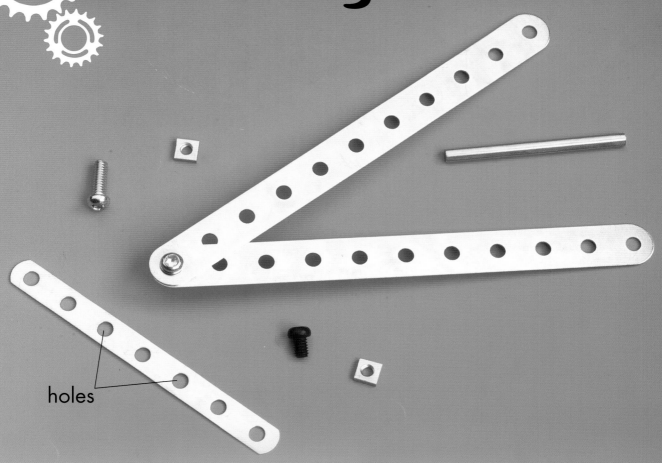

holes

This building toy uses metal pieces with holes in them. The holes are needed to join the pieces together.

Metal pieces come in
many different shapes.
Some of the shapes
connect, or join,
together to build
special models
like this.

Nuts and Bolts

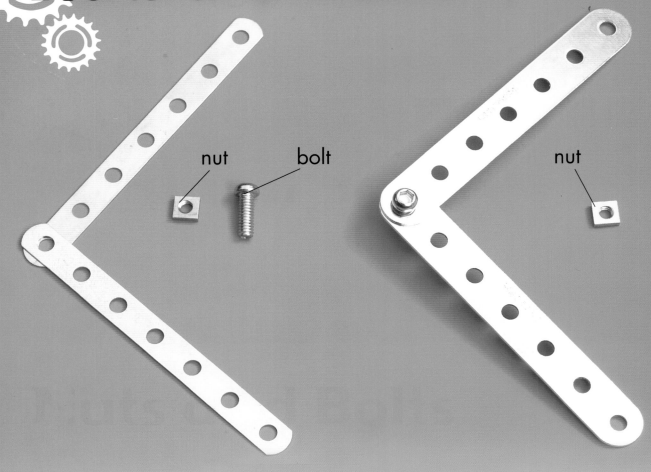

nut   bolt   nut

To join these pieces together you need a **nut** and a **bolt**. You must line up all the holes you want to join up. The bolt is the part that goes through the holes.

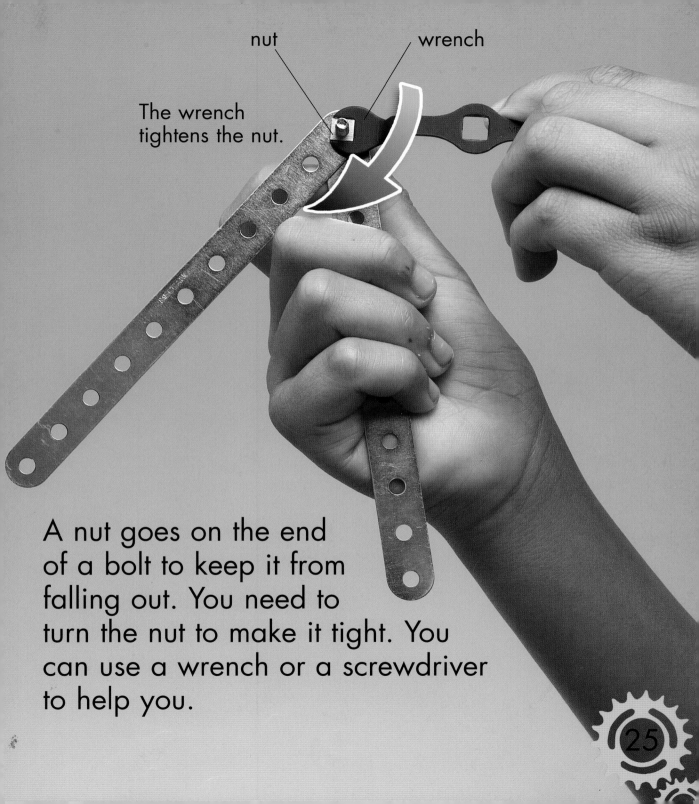

nut   wrench

The wrench
tightens the nut.

A nut goes on the end
of a bolt to keep it from
falling out. You need to
turn the nut to make it tight. You
can use a wrench or a screwdriver
to help you.

25

Models with Motors

motor

wheels

nuts

bolts

Simple metal pieces can be put together with a **motor** to make large models that move.

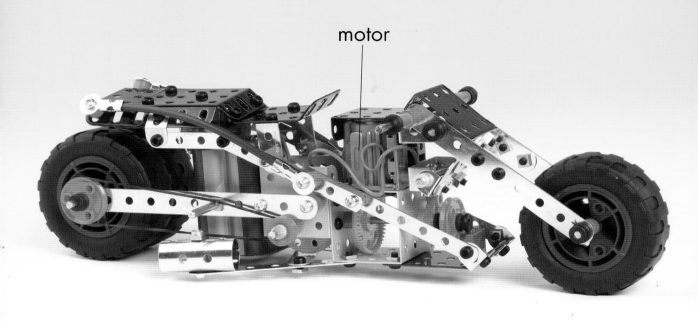

motor

This motorcycle has been built using
wheels, nuts, bolts, and a motor.
The motor makes the wheels
turn and the motorcycle move.

Spot the Difference!

Construction toys can be used to build the most amazing things. One of these photos shows a giant model of New York City, made of plastic bricks. The other is a photo of the real city. Can you tell which is which?

Glossary

axle rod that holds a wheel but still lets the wheel turn around

battery something that stores electricity

bolt metal pin used to hold things together

connector shape that joins two or more rods together

construction building

electricity kind of energy used for lighting, heating, and making machines work

gravity force that pulls everything down toward the ground

motor something that uses electricity or fuel to make a machine move

nut piece of metal with a hole in the middle. It is screwed on to the end of a bolt to hold things together.

pulley wheel used with a string, rope, or chain to make lifting things easier

rod long, thin piece of plastic or metal

More Books to Read

Haslam, Andrew. *Building*. Minnetonka, Minn.: Two-Can Publishing, 2000.

Rathjen, Don. *LEGO Crazy Action Contraptions: A LEGO Ideas Book*. Palo Alto, Calif.: Klutz, 1998.

Wulffson, Don. *Toys! Amazing Stories Behind Some Great Inventions*. New York: Henry Holt and Co., 2000.

Index